TWELVE TOUGH ISSUES—AND MORE

TWELVE TOUGH ISSUES—AND MORE
What the Church Teaches and Why

Archbishop Daniel E. Pilarczyk

ST. ANTHONY MESSENGER PRESS
Cincinnati, Ohio

Library of Congress Cataloging-in-Publication Data

Pilarczyk, Daniel E.
  Twelve tough issues—and more : what the church teaches and
why /
Daniel E. Pilarczyk.
      p. cm.
Rev. ed. of: Twelve tough issues. 1988.
Includes bibliographical references.
  ISBN 0-86716-461-1 (pbk.)
  1. Catholic Church—Doctrines. 2. Church and social
problems—Catholic Church. I. Pilarczyk, Daniel E. Twelve tough
issues.
II. Title.
  BX1751.3 .P55 2002
  230'.2—dc21
                                            2002000292

Cover design by Mark Sullivan

Book design by Sandy L. Digman

ISBN 0-86716-461-1

©2002, Daniel E. Pilarczyk

Published by St. Anthony Messenger Press
www.AmericanCatholic.org
Printed in the U.S.A.

Contents

Preface

These short reflections about the church's moral teaching began as a series of articles in *The Catholic Telegraph*, the official newspaper of the Archdiocese of Cincinnati. It was—and is—my conviction that, if what the church teaches is true and if its acceptance is a matter of our eternal salvation, then it ought to be possible to explain what the church teaches briefly and in a way that ordinary people can understand. You shouldn't have to have a graduate degree in theology to be able to understand and appreciate what God wants us to know and do.

That series of articles was then published as a small book entitled *Twelve Tough Issues*. It has proven useful for RCIA (Rite of Christian Initiation of Adults) programs, for religion classes of various kinds, for adult discussion groups and for individuals in the pursuit of deeper faith and understanding.

Nearly fifteen years have passed since the book's publication, and it seems time for an update. It is not that the church's teaching has changed over these years, but the context in which the teaching is offered is no longer exactly the same as it was then. We have experienced changes of tonality and emphasis in the society in which we live. In addition, new questions have arisen. Also, every human endeavor is capable of improvement.

In view of all that, I now present *Twelve Tough Issues—and More*. All the original chapters have been worked over in varying degrees. The chapter on economics has been rewritten to deal with the wider subject of social justice. I have added new chapters on prolonging life and on church membership. The questions at the end of each chapter have been completely revised to make them sharper. To the chapters on the various issues I have appended some suggestions for further reading. These suggestions include an indication of where the subjects are treated in the *Catechism of the Catholic Church,* as well as material from the writings of Pope John Paul II, the Second Vatican Council, the Holy See and our American bishops' conference. I presume that most Catholics have access to a copy of the *Catechism* and the decrees of the council. For other documentation, I have indicated where it can be found in *Origins,* the weekly documentary service of the bishops' conference, which is available in many parish and public libraries.

I express my gratitude to those who have encouraged me in this endeavor from the beginning until now. May God use these efforts to bring his kingdom a little closer.

Daniel E. Pilarczyk
Archbishop of Cincinnati

Introduction

Trying to listen in the midst of a crowd is tough. Whether we are at a football game, a Thanksgiving Day parade, a protest march or a cocktail party, we have trouble distinguishing who belongs to what voice in a crowd and what the various voices are saying. We hear a mixture of sounds, none distinct. Clarity of sound is hard to get in a crowd, and clarity of meaning even harder.

Yet, we spend much of our lives in crowds. At any given moment a whole chorus of voices surrounds us: voices of the press and the television; voices of the merchants trying to sell us underwear and computers; voices of friends talking about their concerns and their problems; voices of people who disagree with the other voices; and voices within ourselves, deliberating on the personal relevance and worth of what the voices outside us are saying. We live in crowds of voices and sorting them all out is tough.

The purpose of this book is to clarify one of these voices, the voice of the church expressed in official church teaching.

In our culture, the church's voice is one among many; yet, as believers, we hold that the church has something special to say, something of particular importance, indeed, something of eternal importance for our lives. For that reason we need to know what the church is saying amid the vast body of sound that surrounds us. We need to distinguish this voice from the others, simply because this voice is more important than the others.

The church speaks on many issues. In fact, in one way or

another, the church addresses every issue. This is so because the voice of the church reflects the voice of God's love, and God's love affects every aspect of our human existence.

This book, however, will not deal with *all* issues, but only with a few. These few are those that seem most difficult to understand, most difficult to grasp firmly, in the midst of the great clamor in which we spend our lives. I refer to these issues as the "tough issues," tough because of the confusion which surrounds them in our culture, tough because of their inherent complexity, tough because of the demands they make on those who are trying to follow the teaching of the Lord Jesus spoken through his church.

These tough issues include abortion, artificial conception, the prolonging of life, capital punishment, divorce and remarriage, contraception, homosexuality, social justice, warfare, church membership, priestly celibacy, the ordination of women, authority in the church and conscience.

My purpose is not to provide a full theological treatment of each issue. Nor is it to respond to each of the other voices in the crowd, or to answer every possible question. Still less is it to provide weapons to attack those who disagree with the church or those who choose not to listen to its voice. Least of all is it my intent to lay additional guilt on those already burdened by the demands of their lives and their circumstances.

My purpose is simply to identify, clarify and articulate *what* the church teaches about these various matters and *why* the church teaches what it does.

My best hope is that those who read these reflections will better understand and accept what the church teaches and, in the process, come to a deeper realization and acceptance of God's love for us. After all, church teaching is meant to express nothing less than the love of God.

Reality vs. Rules

Before turning to the specific issues, some distinctions in meaning might be helpful.

First, let us distinguish between *teaching* and *rules*.

Teaching has to do with truth, and rules have to do with behavior. Right rules are the practical conclusions from right teaching.

For example, medical science teaches us that smoking is likely to damage our arteries and lungs, thus making us more vulnerable to heart attacks and lung cancer. Scientific research has discovered this truth. It is the way things are. Consequently, doctors tell us that we should not smoke. This is a rule based on the teaching, a precept for behavior based on a reality.

We may not like the rule. We may want to smoke two packs of cigarettes a day. We may demand that the rule be changed. However, demanding that the rule be changed, or simply disregarding the rule, makes no sense unless we can demonstrate that the reality on which the rule is based is false.

The rules for moral behavior that the church offers to us are the same. They are not based on the decision of some ecclesiastical legislator, but on the awareness of a truth, of a reality, which itself determines the behavioral consequences. Demanding that the church change the "rules" is meaningless if the rules reflect reality. The church does not make the reality. It discerns and teaches what the reality is and helps us see the implications for behavior that flow from the reality.

In this book, we will deal primarily with the *realities* from which the *rules* flow.

Harm vs. Sin

We must also distinguish between *doing wrong* and *committing sin*.

Neither we ourselves, nor those around us, nor the church are free to ignore reality or to treat it as if it were something different from what it is. In fact, whenever we behave in a way which conflicts with reality, we do harm: to ourselves, to those around us, to the community of the church.

Moreover, the harm that comes from disregarding the demands of reality is automatic. Whether we are aware of it or not, whether we intend it or not, the harm occurs. If I smoke two packs of cigarettes every day, I harm my body, whether I have ever heard that smoking is harmful. What I am doing is harmful, and therefore wrong, regardless of my ignorance.

Sin is something more than doing wrong. Sin is consciously and deliberately doing what I know to be in disaccord with reality. Sin is doing wrong while knowing I am doing wrong and freely wanting to do the wrong. Because I have free will, I am morally accountable for the sins I commit. They are my responsibility because I have freely and knowingly chosen them. The harm that comes from them is a harm I have freely done.

This distinction between doing wrong and committing sin is an important one because it can keep us from judging the sinfulness of others. If I know and understand the reality that lies behind the church's moral "rules," I may be able to determine that certain courses of behavior that others follow are ultimately harmful and therefore wrong. I may wish to try to help the others see the error of their ways. But I am not authorized to conclude that they are committing sin. That conclusion belongs to God, who alone is able to read hearts and minds and determine what degree of personal responsibility belongs to each choice that people make.

Witnessing vs. Accusing

In this book, my purpose is to bear witness to the wisdom and the love of God. I do not wish to convict anyone of personal sin, nor do I invite others to do so. That task is far too great for our small human resources. I merely wish to identify the realities that underlie the issues in question and to clarify the most important of the many voices that surround us, and give witness to the truth.

We all face tough issues, tough in many ways, tough for many reasons. But even the tough issues can be easier to grasp when we understand the realities behind them. The most basic reality is God's love for human creatures. That love is what this book is about.

Discussion Questions

1. What voices do I perceive in my life offering direction for my actions?

2. Is it easier to do what is right if we know why it is right? Why? Why not?

3. In matters of personal behavior, is it ever better to be ignorant than to be well informed?

CHAPTER ONE

Abortion

Reverence is a fundamental element of religion. Once we acknowledge that God exists and that God is creator and Lord of all that exists, we become aware of our own littleness in comparison to God. We find God at the same time fearsome and fascinating. In relation to God, we find ourselves in a posture of awe and submission. All this we call reverence.

This reverence for God extends to all that is of God. Nothing of the creation that surrounds us is really ours to do with as we please. It is all God's doing. It is all the result of God's loving will. We are called to respect and reverence God's handiwork as we are called to respect and reverence God.

We perceive that God's human creatures are the masterwork of creation, that they have a particular dignity all their own and that, therefore, they have a claim for special reverence. Scripture expresses this by telling us that humankind is created in God's very own image and likeness (Genesis 1:26 ff.). Human life is to be revered and respected because it is a special reflection of the holiness we associate with God. It is sacred.

The Church's View

These fundamental religious insights are the basis for the church's teaching about abortion. No human life, even unborn human life, is ours to do with as we please because all human life is God's. This is the foundation for the claim to inviolability and respect that each of us has the right to expect from other men and women and they from us.

This claim to inviolability and reverence, this human dignity, is prior to all achievement. Human dignity does not depend on human accomplishments or even on human potential. It does not have to be earned. It does not have to be demonstrated. It is a given, a presupposition established by God and therefore beyond all human demands for proof or justification. That which is human has a right to be, simply because it is there, simply because it is God's.

The willful destruction of any innocent human life, born or unborn, is therefore wrong because it is a violation of the rights of God the creator. Killing an innocent human being involves interfering with that which is not ours, treating as our own that which is God's alone. It is an offense against the reverence we owe to God.

This teaching is easy to understand when we are dealing with women and men we can see and know. If we look closely enough, we can see some worth in practically anybody, a worth that precedes any conferring of rights by human agency. To see human dignity in one who is yet to be born is less easy. Yet, experts in genetics assure us that unborn babies are as human as we are. Consequently, human dignity and worth are there. The unborn belong to God in the same way and to the same degree that each of us belongs to God.

All this explains why people of religious conviction find the killing of an unborn child abhorrent.

From a religious point of view, then, abortion is not a particularly tough issue. Abortion is obviously wrong, and the reasons are clear. Abortion becomes a tough issue, however, in the context of a society that does not accept religious argumentation.

A Secular View

Are there purely rational grounds for opposing abortion in a secular context that makes no provision for religious beliefs as such? Yes, there are. Any society that permits the general killing of unborn children runs the risk of eventual self-destruction. Such a society launches a logic that leads to social suicide.

The basic protection that society must provide its citizens is the protection of the right to be. Our Declaration of Independence expresses as self-evident the truths "that all men are created equal, that they are endowed by their Creator with certain unalienable rights, that among these are life, liberty and the pursuit of happiness," and that governments are instituted to secure these rights. Whether one believes in a creator or not, the responsibility of government in the matter of human life is clear.

When abortion was legalized in our country, government, in effect, said that the unalienable right to life does not apply to certain beings that are, nonetheless, definitely *human* beings. A whole class was eliminated from the law's protection. For all practical purposes, it put every unborn child legally at risk.

In doing this, government posed a threat against us all. If unborn human beings can be left legally unprotected, what about human beings at the other end of life: the terminally ill, the senile, those who have lived out their "usefulness"? What about those who seem not to fit in with the rest of society? What about those who are, for whatever reason, unpopular? If society can take away the protection of life from one group, it can take that protection away from us all. Here we are dealing not with theology but with simple logic.

Legalizing abortion turned a crime into a right. It was a judicial and social mistake, a grave mistake that we must find a way to remedy if our country is to preserve its very foundation. The question to be faced here is not *whether* a reversal of our country's position on abortion is called for but *how* that reversal is to be achieved. The most direct way to effect the change would be through an amendment to our Constitution which would prohibit all abortions at all times for any reason. Another approach, recognizing the political obstacles to a constitutional amendment, would be to entrust the matter of abortion to the individual states' legislatures in the hope that positions respectful of human life may be easier to bring to legal expression there than at the federal level.

But what level of popular support would be required to make either of these approaches effective? If, by hypothesis, an amendment were to be passed which large groups of people found unacceptable, would we be opening the door to the kind of lawlessness our country experienced under Prohibition? A change of heart is as necessary as a change of the law.

Large numbers of our fellow citizens seem to be opposed to abortion on demand but think abortion should be allowed in certain circumstances. Could or should abortion legally be tolerated in some cases where morality clearly forbids it? How much moral evil should a society allow for the sake of a greater good? Is it better to legalize all abortions, or to permit abortion only in the extremely rare cases of pregnancy resulting from rape or incest while forbidding all the rest? These are issues on which persons of good will differ, even if they agree that the moral and societal implications of abortion are such that a change of our present policy is imperative.

An Individual Challenge

Abortion is also a tough issue at the level of the individual. This is not the place to consider in detail the subjective situation of the woman who decides to get an abortion, except to remark that sometimes the decision is made in panic and desperation. That does not make it a right decision, of course, but it reminds us that Christian love and compassion are not offered only to those who have never made a wrong choice. Many dioceses have programs to assist women who want to deal with the moral and psychological aftermath of an abortion.

All of us need to address many complicated questions as we come to grips with abortion. What steps can I, as an individual, take to change this destructive direction in which our society is heading? Is it acceptable to do nothing? If not, is it acceptable to do everything? Are any and all means appropriate as long as the end is good? What is my obligation as a

Christian believer toward those who provide abortion services? What kind of support can or should I provide to those who offer national and local leadership in opposing abortion? Is opposition to abortion a matter of protest only, or must there also be a component of assistance to those who find themselves in a difficult situation? What alternatives to abortion are there, and how can these alternatives be made available to those who need them? What is the role of social and moral education in all this?

Plenty of questions are connected with abortion. Some have clear and cogent answers; others do not. Clearly, the issue here is a tough one. The way we address it will be determined by our love for our country and our reverence for the human dignity that comes to each of us from God.

Discussion Questions

1. If the law gives women "the right to choose" an abortion, how does that affect the morality of abortion?

2. Should even a nonreligious person oppose abortion? Why? How?

3. Is it right to settle for a law that would permit abortion in the rare cases of pregnancy resulting from rape or incest, or must we press for a law that would outlaw all abortions?

4. What have I done to oppose abortion?

For Further Reading

Catechism of the Catholic Church, 2270–2275.

Pope John Paul II, Encyclical Letter *Evangelium Vitae,* 1995, nos. 58–63 (*Origins* 24:42).

National Conference of Catholic Bishops, "Resolution on Abortion," November 1989 (*Origins* 19:24).

Chapter Two

Artificial Conception

Just a few decades ago, the laboratory production of human life was not a tough moral issue. It was science fiction.

Things have changed. Scientists can now fertilize human eggs in a laboratory dish, implant some in the mother and freeze the rest for future use. They can transfer a naturally fertilized egg from one woman to another, farming out, as it were, the gestation of the child. It will not be long before scientists will be able to produce a human being by cloning.

Today, doctors can determine which marriage partner is the source of a couple's inability to have children. If the condition impeding conception cannot be remedied, it can often be sidestepped by using the contracted services of someone outside the marriage. Prominent human males offer their sperm to women who hope to conceive a child prodigy. Couples can produce human fetuses as sources of biological material for the physical well-being of others, often their other children.

Our moral reaction to many of these issues is instinctive, quick and sound. The insemination of a woman with the sperm of a man other than her husband is tantamount to adultery, even if both she and her husband consent to the procedure. Recent court cases about surrogate motherhood illustrate that the psychological and social problems of one woman carrying another's fetus to term, for pay or for free, are so great that surrogate motherhood is clearly unacceptable and that to beget a fetus solely for the purpose of using it to provide human spare parts is morally monstrous. Few would dispute such things.

Why do we spontaneously agree on such things being wrong? What principles do we apply here?

Underlying Principles

One principle is the dignity of the human being. As creatures made in God's image, human beings are not objects to be disposed of as another human sees fit, nor are we objects to be generated as another sees fit. Human beings are not objects at all, but inviolable creatures of a loving God. When we employ our scientific expertise to channel the processes of human generation into artificial productivity, we are doing something that is not ours to do.

A second principle is respect for marriage. Marriage is not the casual coupling of two people for purposes of interpersonal sociability or for the production of human bodies. It is the foundation of a family, a family that originates from the love shared between husband and wife and expressed in sexual union. Every human being has the right to be born as the result of such a loving union, and every human being has the right to be born in a human way. To permit or procure anything else reduces the marriage partners to the status of consumers and the offspring to the level of a product which consumers desire, shop for and buy.

A third principle has to do with "can do" versus "may do." The scientific capacity to do something does not make that something morally right. Medical science does not have the right to do something simply because that something is now doable. Moral criteria apply to science and to scientific research just as moral criteria apply to every other human activity. The basic moral criterion that applies to artificial conception (as to abortion) is respect for the dignity of human life—which is not ours to do with as we please and which is greater than the desire of individuals either to destroy or to produce. Human life is not an object like other objects. Just as human life is not a by-product to be thrown away, so also it is not a product to be manufactured.

This is relatively easy to understand when we are dealing with obviously inhuman and unsocial procedures to artificially generate human life, procedures which involve non-spouses or the commercialization of human life. But other situations involving the artificial conception of human life seem less morally clear to many. What about a husband and wife, unable to conceive, who desperately desire children and who wish to try a procedure that involves only the two of them? What principles are involved here?

The basic principle is that any medical procedure which sets out merely to facilitate the sexual act and assist it to arrive at its purpose is morally acceptable. Thus, the medical transfer of an egg around a blockage in a Fallopian tube presents no moral problem. The procedure merely overcomes the body's deficiencies while respecting the nature of loving human intercourse.

To Help, Not Replace, Intercourse

However, procedures designed not to help the natural act but to substitute for it are morally different, even when the participants are loving spouses. An example of such a substitution is *in vitro* fertilization of a wife's egg by her husband's sperm outside her body. What is at issue here is not a loving personal union of husband and wife, but something else: a kind of artificial intercourse takes the place of the loving human contact through which children are naturally conceived.

This is a difficult part of the church's teaching for many people to understand. This is where principles give rise to tough questions. The answers are not the kind that compel immediate assent, but they do invoke the same principles that are applied to the other examples of artificial conception.

"Don't parents have a right to have children if they want them?" No, they don't. A child is not an object to be owned. Neither a child nor the right to bear a child "belong" to the parents. A human life is always God's. A human life is always a gift.

"What difference does it make how the couple goes about conceiving as long as the intentions are loving and right?" The difference lies in what we are saying by our human actions. If we confine ourselves to the natural act of intercourse or to procedures that remove the defects of this natural act, our actions say that we respect the demands of human dignity and human inviolability. We are giving witness to a certain "untouchable" element in human existence that pertains not only to existing human life, but also to the processes by which human life comes to be. If we engage in procedures that bypass or substitute for the natural act of human generation, we are saying that human life is ours to control by any means at our disposal.

"Is it wrong for couples without children to want to conceive?" No, it is not wrong, but a goal's goodness does not justify every means that might be used to pursue that goal.

This teaching is hard for childless couples to accept. But we all have to keep in mind that the church's purpose in this teaching is not to inflict pain or demonstrate insensitivity but to be consistent in its attitude toward human life. We must respect the dimension of radical inviolability inherent in human life. When there is any question about what is appropriate, the decision has to be made in favor of human dignity. We are dealing not with a commodity, not with an object, but with a creature of God created in God's image and likeness.

The many approaches to artificial conception in our culture make it a tough issue. So do its increased availability and use. But the basic church teaching is about human dignity and about the lordship of God. To the extent we disregard that teaching, we place ourselves at risk by trivializing the human life on which rests our own personal inviolability and human dignity.

The childless couple who must make a moral decision about artificial conception find themselves in moral tension. On the one hand, their love for one another and for potential children demonstrates respect for humanity. On the other, this respect for humanity, for the inviolable dignity of the human person, constitutes the moral restraint that keeps them from engaging in inappropriate means to carry out their desire. The basic dignity of every human person takes precedence over the wishes of the couple, however laudable those wishes may be.

In the matter of artificial conception there are social, legal and moral questions. The answers to some are obvious; the answers to others are harder to see. But beneath all the puzzlement and pain lie the love of God for human creatures and the dignity that love imparts.

Discussion Questions

1. What kinds of artificial conception techniques are available in my community? Is there any discussion or question about their moral acceptability?

2. What social outcomes are to be foreseen as artificial conception becomes readily available and commonly practiced?

3. What morally acceptable options do married couples have who want children but have been unable to conceive?

For Further Reading

Catechism of the Catholic Church, 2374–2379.

Congregation for the Doctrine of the Faith, *Instruction on Respect for Human Life,* 1987 (*Origins* 16:40).

National Conference of Catholic Bishops, *Ethical and Religious Directives for Catholic Health Care Services,* 2001, nos. 38–43 (*Origins* 24:27).

CHAPTER THREE

Prolonging Life

It should be clear by now that Catholic faith regards human life as a gift, as something entrusted to us by God which we are called to respect and defend, which we are not permitted to do with as we please.

From this it follows that euthanasia, the deliberate and intentional termination of a human life when that life is perceived to be burdensome or nonproductive, is wrong. It is the same thing as murder. Human life is not ours to end whenever we see fit, and a human life that has become painful or less pleasurable than it once was still remains God's gift, still remains precious.

Asking or allowing physicians to assist in terminating human life for persons who are suffering physical or mental illness is to involve them in behavior that is totally opposed to their calling to heal and comfort.

Taking Care of Ourselves

From the Catholic Christian view of life it also follows that individuals have the responsibility to care for the health of their bodies. If our bodily life is a gift of God, given us on loan to use in accord with God's will for us, we have to look after it and protect it and nourish it. God does not expect us to become hypochondriacs and spend every waking moment being concerned about our health, but he does expect us to take ordinary care of ourselves: to eat regularly, to keep ourselves clean, to go to the doctor when we are sick or injured, to take the medicine and carry out the treatment that is prescribed for us. This is a matter of ongoing maintenance and of keeping ourselves in good repair.

Does that mean that we have to do anything and everything the doctors tell us, no matter what? Are we obliged to do every conceivable thing to keep ourselves alive? The answer to both questions is no. Our human life is indeed a gift of God, a gift that we are called to respect and care for. But it is not the only, nor the final, gift that God has given us. We believe that our life on this earth is a preparation for something better, for the whole new kind of living that involves happiness and fulfillment in the company of God forever. That does not make life on this earth any less precious, but it makes the worth and value of earthly life relative and secondary to the final state that God has in store for us. Hence we are not obliged to maintain our present earthly life at all costs, as if there were nothing more in store for us.

Principles for Choices

As church leaders and theologians have reflected on the implications of our responsibility to take care of our earthly life, they have been able to formalize a set of principles about what is expected of us in this context.

First, we are to take care of our health. We are obliged to take advantage of the usual and readily available measures that people ordinarily use to stay healthy or to get well when they are sick or injured.

Second, we are not obliged to use medical measures that do not contribute to our getting better or that are excessively burdensome to the patient or to those people closely associated with the patient. These kinds of medical measures are known as "extraordinary" or "disproportionate." They include treatments that are risky or experimental, treatments that are excessively painful, as well as treatments that do not make the patient any better but only maintain him or her in a present state of incapacity when there is no hope for recovery.

Nor are we obliged to undergo treatments that we would find excessively burdensome or that would impose excessive burdens on our families. For example, if the situation requires driving fifty or a hundred miles each day with a family member to get treatments, most people would agree that one would not be obliged to take those treatments.

Deciding what we are going to do in contexts like this is not easy. This is a tough issue. We have to weigh very carefully our obligation to care for our human health against the burdens that certain kinds of health care might impose on us. In the same set of circumstances, different people might make different decisions.

The principles just outlined are part of standard Catholic moral teaching. But there is another question that is still under study and is disputed among Catholic ethicists. It is the question of nutrition and hydration (that is, providing food and water) for terminally ill patients. If a patient is clearly not going to get better and if food and water are now being provided by feeding tubes or intravenous drips, is the patient obliged to continue these procedures in spite of their inconvenience and clear lack of long-term benefit? For that matter, if the patient is unconscious and is likely to remain so indefinitely, may the patient's family decide to terminate the nutrition and hydration procedures?

Those who say that the procedures may be terminated hold that these kinds of nutrition and hydration are medical procedures and that the same rules apply to them that apply to other medical procedures. Those who say that the procedures may not be terminated hold that nutrition and hydration are basic human rights and must continue to be provided as long as the patient is alive.

It seems clear that the presumption should be in favor of providing nutrition and hydration unless the patient finds them excessively painful or burdensome.

Difficulties

These are all tough issues. Most people seem not to want to have their life prolonged with a whole kaleidoscope of tubes and needles and medications if it really is not going to do them any good. Yet we all have responsibilities for taking care of and maintaining our human life. It is not morally acceptable to opt out of our life at the first sign of any suffering or malady. Likewise, these decisions are not just personal decisions that we can make all by ourselves. They require information from medical personnel, input from family and friends, and generally some spiritual guidance to assure that the decisions being made are reasonable and in accord with human dignity. The issues become even tougher when the patient is no longer able to make decisions and others must take the responsibility to decide.

There is still another dimension to these matters that makes them seem difficult and dangerous. If I am allowed to forego medical treatment that is useless or burdensome and this leads to my death, have I committed suicide? Are all these distinctions merely a disguise for euthanasia? How can we call ourselves pro-life if we are teaching people that it is all right in certain circumstances to allow themselves to die?

In response to these questions, we have to be clear about what we are doing. We are not killing people nor teaching people that they can kill themselves. We are simply saying that we do not have to maintain our human life at all costs and that in certain extreme circumstances, it is permissible to let nature take its course. Letting someone die is not the same as making someone die.

This kind of approach to the prolongation of life does not include disrespect for life. Rather, it gives witness to our belief that, beyond this human life so wonderful and so precious, there is something more that is better still and that, although we are not allowed to open the door to eternity for ourselves, we are permitted to go through the door when the Lord opens it for us.

Discussion Questions

1. Have I ever had to make life-or-death decisions about my own health care? What criteria did I use to make those decisions?

2. Why do many people seem not to want to be kept alive indefinitely if they are not lucid?

3. What kind of health care would I find excessively burdensome for me? For my family?

4. Have I identified persons to help me with health care decisions or to make decisions for me if I am unable to do so?

For Further Reading

Catechism of the Catholic Church, 2278–2279.

Congregation for the Doctrine of the Faith, *Declaration on Euthanasia*, 1980 (*Origins* 10:10).

Pope John Paul II, Encyclical Letter *Evangelium Vitae*, 1995, no. 65 (*Origins* 24:42).

National Conference of Catholic Bishops, *Ethical and Religious Directives for Catholic Health Care Services*, 2001, nos. 56–61 (*Origins* 31:9).

CHAPTER FOUR

Capital Punishment

Capital punishment is a tough issue because our teaching seems contradictory. On the one hand, Christian faith maintains that all human life is sacred, that it is God's to give and take, not ours. Yet traditional Christian teaching has also held that executing convicted criminals is permissible. Now, in the last decade or so, the pope is teaching that capital punishment should be abolished. What is going on here?

To understand these seeming contradictions we must begin by identifying correctly the questions at issue. There are two: (1) Does society have the right to terminate the life of those who have, through legal process, been convicted of serious crimes? (2) Even if society has the right, should it exercise this right?

Society's Right

The answer to the first question is yes. Saint Thomas Aquinas, speaking about the crime of deliberate murder, formulated the traditional teaching: "If a person is dangerous and destructive to the community on account of some sin, it is praiseworthy and healthy that he be killed in order that the common good be preserved" (*Summa* 2a2ae, 64.2). That's pretty clear!

We are dealing here with the question of self-defense. If a person is so violent and so vicious that human society itself is threatened, society has the right, if necessary, to take that person's life in order to preserve itself.

Human life, all human life, is indeed sacred—the life of the sinner, but also the life of the innocent. Precisely for this reason, innocent persons are permitted to defend themselves from the convicted criminal. There is no obligation to sacrifice the life of the innocent for the sake of the life of a social offender who threatens to destroy the innocent. Just as I have an obligation to defend my life against its destruction by disease, so also I have an obligation—or at least a right—to defend my life against its destruction by malefactors. If this were not the case, all human society would degenerate into a struggle for mere survival, or into domination by those who are most violent. Society's taking the life of the convicted criminal is not denying the inviolability of human life, but rather asserting the inviolability of human life against those who would destroy it.

Society's Need

This brings us to the second question at issue: Given society's right to take the criminal's life, should it do so? Here the answer is both yes and no. Yes, if taking the life of the criminal is the only way that society can defend itself against destruction. No, if society can defend itself in some other way. In other words, the presumption in favor of human life takes precedence if the well-being of society is not endangered.

Church leaders (including Pope John Paul II) who advocate the abolition of the death penalty believe that society no longer needs to defend itself by means of capital punishment. We are no longer in a semi-barbarous frontier situation in which the lives and livelihoods of innocent citizens are at the mercy of lawless people who cannot be restrained except by execution. We have other ways of dealing with lawless people. We no longer need to take their lives to defend ourselves and, because we do not need to take life, we should not.

In addition to that basic insight, other factors argue against the necessity or wisdom of inflicting capital punishment:

• Many potential criminals are not deterred by the threat of

the death penalty.
• The death penalty is carried out on an entirely disproportionate number of poor persons and minorities. This is not
because the well-to-do abstain from violent crimes but because the well-to-do can provide better legal defense for
themselves.

• Miscarriages of justice do occur. Erroneous executions take
place and, obviously, cannot be rectified.

In summary, while society always has the right to defend itself
against those who would destroy it, exercising the right to ex-
ecute criminals is no longer necessary, useful or just. The basic
principle has not changed, but its application, appropriate in
other social contexts, is not appropriate in our culture and
time.

Several other matters call for comment in connection with
capital punishment.

Punishment—Not Revenge

First, the exercise of capital punishment should never have
been a matter of revenge and cannot morally ever be a matter
of revenge. Someone's having done an evil to me never gives
me the right to do evil back in order to make that person suffer as I have suffered. The biblical directive about "eye for eye
and tooth for tooth" (Exodus 21:24) calls for evildoers to be
punished, but is also intended to protect offenders from un-
limited revenge. It sets a maximum punishment. It does not legitimate vindictiveness.

Second, the case against capital punishment is not a case
against all punishment. Those who have harmed society must
be made to provide some recompense to society. In most cases,
this involves removing them from the community through imprisonment, taking away their freedom. Ideally, imprisonment
gives the offender a chance to repent and undergo rehabilita-
tion. Given the realities of the penal system in our country,
however, this is often not the case. Nonetheless, imprisonment
does punish the criminal by taking him or her out of the kind

of social existence that constitutes humane living for most people. Anyone who has ever visited a maximum-security prison will agree that incarcerated criminals are not eluding punishment!

Third, Catholic leaders who oppose capital punishment and who call for its abolition are not denying traditional teaching. They are, rather, giving guidance about the application of traditional teaching in its fullness to the concrete circumstances in which we live. They are making a judgment about how traditional moral principles seem to find application here and now. Such a judgment is not an infallible dogmatic teaching but an exercise of pastoral leadership and so calls for our acceptance. Persons of good will may disagree with the position, given the complexities of all social questions. But if they are to disagree conscientiously, they must take into account the purpose of the basic teaching and the realities of our society.

Another question inherent in the issue of capital punishment concerns our own attitudes toward social offenders. Obviously we are not free to hate them or anyone else; we believe that the Lord calls on his followers to love everyone, even their enemies.

At the same time, we must feel compassion for those whose lives have been irreparably harmed, or even taken, by the antisocial behavior of the criminal offender. We dare not pretend that nothing has happened, that the victims have no claim on society or that forgiveness is easy. Nor may we allow our society to be undermined by lawlessness.

We are dealing here with a tough issue of reconciling rights: the rights of all those who would live peaceably in the human community as well as the rights of the offenders. There are no easy answers, but we know that we cannot solve moral and social problems by rough and ready solutions which do not really speak to the complexities of the situations to which they are addressed.

In the final analysis, we are dealing with the problem of finding and expressing the love of God for us human creatures even in the context of human crime. And that is a tough issue.

Discussion Questions

1. Why do so many Catholics seem to favor capital punishment?

2. Is there any significance to the fact that the United States executes proportionately many more criminals than any other country?

3. What attitudes toward social offenders are appropriate from a Christian standpoint? What attitudes are inappropriate?

For Further Reading

Catechism of the Catholic Church, 2265–2267.

Pope John Paul II, Encyclical Letter *Evangelium Vitae,* 1995, nos. 55–56 (*Origins* 16:40).

United States Catholic Conference, *Statement on Capital Punishment,* 1980 (*Origins* 10:24).

CHAPTER FIVE

Divorce and Remarriage

D ivorce and remarriage by Catholics may be the toughest issue of all because it affects so many people. Is there anyone who does not have friends or family who married in the church, then divorced and remarried? These situations are painful for those who have experienced the breakup of their marriages as well as their families and friends and, especially, their children.

This is not the place to offer a complete treatment of the church's teaching about marriage and the sacrament of matrimony. But we can address certain aspects of this difficult issue in order to make the church's teaching more understandable.

Human Ideal as Christian Norm

Most important is what the church means by sacramental marriage. A sacramental marriage is the establishment of a complete partnership of life and love between two baptized persons, each free and competent to marry, which takes place in the context of the church community. The church believes, based on Scripture, that such a marriage is something more than an agreement between two people. The church sees sacramental marriage as a reflection of Christ's love for his church. When a man and a woman pledge lifelong faithfulness to each other within the community of faith, they pledge themselves to mirror to the community the unconditional faithfulness which exists between the Lord Jesus and his people. If the rest of us want to know to what degree Christ will remain in touch with us, to what degree he will continue to love us, we are invited to look at the love of husband and wife in Christian marriage. In a sacramental marriage, the spouses pledge their married lives to make that statement. They commit their married lives to teach the church about Christ's love. Because Christ's love is permanent, so is Christian marriage.

Even apart from Christian faith, permanent, indissoluble marriage is clearly the ideal from a natural perspective. For a woman and man to love each other so much that they give their whole lives to each other is a profound reflection of human greatness. It is unquestionably appropriate that children be born into the context of that kind of love; that they be brought to maturity and learn to be fully human in the light of the example of their parents' love for each other; that children learn to appreciate human generosity by experiencing the self-sacrifice and devotion of parents and grandparents.

In obedience to the teaching of Jesus (see, for example, Mark 10,11 ff.), the church takes this natural ideal and makes it the norm for believers, seeing in it a reflection of nothing less than Christ's love for each of us. For the church to teach that sacramental marriages can be dissolved and that the divorced spouses can properly enter into subsequent marriages would be to teach that Christ's love for us can disintegrate, that there is provision for inconstancy in it, that perhaps he does not love us unconditionally and forever.

Human reality, however, is not quite so neat. Sometimes a married couple find that they are simply unable to carry out their commitments to one another. (This is, of course, not the same as simply losing interest in one another or finding the marriage a matter of inconvenience.) Circumstances develop which make it impossible, sometimes even destructive, for them to live together as wife and husband. Often it becomes a matter of impossibility, and they break up their common life. What then?

Annulment vs. Divorce

As we consider what happens in such a situation, it is necessary to make some distinctions about marriages and about the relationship of the divorced spouses to the community of the church.

Sometimes the parties in the marriage were simply incapable, from the beginning, of giving themselves to one another in a full communion of life and love. Perhaps deep psychological problems prevented it. Perhaps one spouse entered the marriage under the influence of fear, to a degree that his or her consent was not really free. Or it may be that, in spite of appearances, one of the parties did not in fact give himself or herself to the kind of unconditional relationship that is required for sacramental marriage, not intending, for example, to enter a lifetime commitment or deliberately excluding the intention to be faithful to the other partner. In such cases, what seemed to be a sacramental marriage can be submitted to the judgment of the church, which, through its matrimonial tribunal, may ascertain that a real, valid, sacramental marriage never existed.

From the beginning, what seemed to be an image of the love of Christ for his church was not so, because of the situation of one or both of the spouses. The church tribunal will then issue a "declaration of nullity," a judicial pronouncement that acknowledges there never was a sacramental marriage. This is not some kind of subtle "Catholic divorce" proceeding. A declaration of nullity is simply a discernment of the truth of the situation of the persons in what appeared to have been a sacramental marriage. When such a judgment has been pronounced, the parties are free to marry again, not because something which formerly existed has been dissolved, but because no sacramental marriage ever existed. (It may be worth noting that, although the church may find that no sacramental marriage bond ever existed, the children of such a union are not considered illegitimate.)

Sometimes, however, the tribunal process reveals that a sacramental marriage was contracted. There were no obstacles, the parties did freely and totally give themselves to one another, everything in the marriage was as it seemed to be and should have been. But as time went by, the husband and wife grew apart. Perhaps there was unfaithfulness or other fault on the part of one spouse or both. Psychologically the love they had for one another is gone. They obtain a civil divorce. But their responsibilities toward the church remain. In the context of faith, they are unable to enter another sacramental marriage, because they are still bound by the pledge of faithfulness to each other that they made to Christ and the church. Because they gave themselves to each other to be a sign of the faithfulness of Christ, they are bound to continue to reflect that faithfulness in their lives. If they are unable to reflect it in their life together, they are called to respect it in their life apart, without attempting another marriage union.

Still Members of the Church

Sometimes people are confused about the status in the church of married persons who do not live together as husband and wife. (We are talking here about those whose marriages were and are sacramentally valid, not about those whose marriages have been declared null from the beginning by a church tribunal.)

Those who have obtained a civil divorce and who have not remarried are not excluded from the reception of Holy Communion. Perhaps they need to seek forgiveness for whatever fault was theirs in the breakup of the common life of the marriage. But when they have done so, the full life of the church is at their disposal.

Those who have obtained a civil divorce and who have attempted another marriage in civil law have freely put themselves in a morally wrong relationship by living with a person who is not their spouse. For that reason they may not receive Holy Communion as long as they remain in such a relationship. It is not that the church singles out invalidly married people for special punishment. *All* church members who deliberately remain in sinful situations are ineligible to receive Communion. But such persons are not therefore excluded from membership in the church. They are free to participate in the life of the church to the extent that their situation allows.

"But why can't the church be more compassionate?" people sometimes ask. "Why can't the church offer people forgiveness for their mistakes and let them get on with their lives?" For one thing, the church is not free to downplay or disregard the dimension of marriage which reflects Christ's love and faithfulness to us. The church is not free to disregard this dimension, because the church did not put it there. Christ did. For the church to downplay or overlook the demand for total, unconditional and lifelong commitment which is central to sacramental marriage would make the church itself unfaithful to Christ. For another, no sin can be forgiven unless the sinner is willing to forgo the sin, to get out of the sinful situation that he or she has gotten into.

Most of us are familiar with marriage situations that do not admit of apparent resolution. The continuance of common life does not seem possible. No grounds exist to declare that the marriage was null from the beginning. Human needs cry out to be satisfied. There seems to be a conflict between compassion and the demands of faithfulness. What we do then is turn to the cross of Christ and acknowledge that our faithfulness can be very costly, even as his was, and that the love of God for us human creatures is sometimes expressed in a call to suffering and sacrifice.

Discussion Questions

1. Why is the permanence of marriage not valued and upheld in our culture?

2. Why do so many marriages end in divorce?

3. What options are open to a Catholic whose marriage is crumbling and who wishes to remain faithful to church teaching?

For Further Reading

Catechism of the Catholic Church, 1621–1632, 1643–1654.

Pope John Paul II, Apostolic Exhortation *Familiaris Consortio,* 1981, nos. 79–84 (*Origins* 11:28 and 29).

National Conference of Catholic Bishops, *Faithful for Life,* 1995 (*Origins* 25:7).

CHAPTER SIX

Contraception

What does the church teach about birth control? The church's teaching is offered in the context of its teaching about marriage. Marriage was instituted by God as a lifetime communion of a man and woman who give themselves totally, definitively and exclusively to one another as a reflection of God's love for his people, Christ's love for the church. Therefore, marriage must reflect not only self-gift in love but also fruitfulness. Just as God's love is not limiting and restrictive but live-giving and creative, so also marriage is a community of openness to life as well as a community of two persons' love for one another. Marriage cannot be introverted (turned only inward) any more than the love and care of God are introverted.

Love-giving and Life-giving

This relationship between husband and wife, with all that it implies, is expressed in sexual intercourse. Sexual relations, then, are intended to express both the love of wife and husband for one another as well as their openness to extending that love to children. Marital intercourse is intended to be both love-giving and life-giving. Shared love and openness to life are the two values, the two basic gifts, inherent in marriage and its sexual expression. Married persons cannot be faithful to the meaning of their marriage if they deliberately suppress either of these values.

This connection of values has many implications: that sexual activity is not exclusively for the benefit of the participants; that sexual relations which do not take into account or which deliberately exclude the possibility of new life are wrong; that sexual relations, even within marriage, which are not an authentic expression of the love of the partners for one another are also wrong.

Does the church, therefore, teach that married couples must have as many children as they can? No. The church teaches that the number and timing of children in a marriage is a decision which belongs to the husband and wife, and to them alone. They have to weigh their circumstances, their own material and psychological resources. In doing so, they must take into account not just their own personal preferences, but also their responsibilities to their extended families, to society and to the church.

Some couples may well decide that their circumstances are such that they can and should have a large family. Others, while respecting the nature of married life, may decide that they should have few children. The essential thing is that the decision not be based on selfish wants but on concerns which are wider than the couple's private community of life. All marriages, even childless ones, must reach out beyond the two partners.

Natural or Artificial?

If family planning is acceptable, what difference does it make whether the means used are natural or artificial?

A virtuous purpose does not automatically justify every means that can be employed in the pursuit of the purpose. The way in which we go about doing something good must itself be good. The end does not justify the means. (One might observe that using good means for a wrong purpose is also unjustified. Thus, the use of natural means to limit children for a completely selfish purpose is also an offense against marriage.)

More is at issue here than a seemingly theoretical question

of means and ends. The difference between natural family planning and contraception lies in what is said by our actions. To practice contraception says that one of the basic values of marriage is ours to do with as we please, that we can deliberately suppress one of the two gifts that are inherent in marriage. It is to take control over something that is not ours to control and try to remake marriage to a pattern other than God's. Natural family planning, on the other hand, even if its outcomes are as effective as the use of contraceptives, gives witness that both the marriage community and the generation of new life are God's gift. Natural family planning is a sign of respect for God's creative lordship.

We are dealing here with more than a theological quibble or a biological fundamentalism. We are dealing with an acknowledgment of our own creaturehood at the deepest levels of personality and personal relationship.

But does natural family planning work? No method of family planning is foolproof. Nobody guarantees the total effectiveness of any contraceptive, and nobody guarantees the total effectiveness of natural family planning. But recent scientific progress in the realm of natural family planning indicates that it can be as effective as practically any contraceptive if properly used.

Some people are skeptical about natural family planning because they associate it with methods now long outdated. To attribute to contemporary methods the same weaknesses as existed in methods practiced twenty years ago is incorrect.

Another difficulty people find with natural family planning is that it requires a certain degree of expertise and discipline. You have to know how to arrive at the information you need, and you have to be willing to use that information in accord with what you are trying to achieve. But this is not to say that you have to have a doctorate in biology or the self-restraint of a monk in order to make it work. Moreover, family planning experts testify that natural family planning prompts whole new dimensions of communication and bonding in married couples.

Objective Evil vs. Personal Sin

Is practicing contraception a sin? Contraception is wrong. It is wrong because of what it says about the basic meaning of the marriage relationship. Its sinfulness depends on the knowledge and freedom of those who practice it. Sometimes personal culpability is reduced by circumstances of fear or confusion or lack of understanding. Sometimes the practice of contraception can be a lesser evil. But contraception is never good.

This does not mean that those who practice contraception are automatically out of the church. It does mean that they need to examine their motives and their actions carefully and keep trying to move toward a more authentically Christian understanding and expression of the love-giving and life-giving significance of their marriage. Simply deciding what one wants to do is not the answer.

What about the world population problem? Doesn't that call for expanding the availability of contraceptives? Most people would agree that we do not have a quick and complete answer to the question of ever-increasing population. Some things do seem to be clear, however. First, increasing the standard of living reduces population growth. Thus, the population question is as much one of economic development as of numbers. Second, when it comes to food, we presently seem to be dealing with a problem of distribution rather than of absolute scarcity. Third, solutions which do not respect human dignity are not answers, attractive as they may seem in the short term. In the long run, they may prove to be self-defeating. These include sterilization and abortion (forced and elective), the dissemination of contraceptives and the presumption that less developed peoples cannot learn natural methods of family planning.

When all the questions have been asked, and answers offered, the fact remains that contraception is a tough issue. There are many reasons why. The economic and social situations in which many couples find themselves are not conducive to having large families and often threaten the very foundations of the family relationship. The insights into human sexuality we have gained over the last half-century or so bring with them new problems and new questions. Our culture would have us believe that regular sexual activity is absolutely necessary for human happiness and that the postponement of satisfaction is unhealthy if not impossible. The traditional teachings of the church about married sexuality have been called into question to the point that what used to be a source of security and clarity is now a source of confusion for many.

Where does the solution lie? Surely in striving to recognize and respect within the toughness of the issue the gifts of the God who is in love with us human creatures.

Discussion Questions

1. Does the fact that the church's teaching about contraception is countercultural mean that it is wrong?

2. Am I well informed about contemporary methods of natural family planning?

3. Is our society supportive of families?

For Further Reading

Catechism of the Catholic Church, 2366–2372.

Pope John Paul II, Apostolic Constitution *Familiaris Consortio*, 1981, nos. 28–35 (*Origins* 11:28 and 29).

CHAPTER SEVEN

Homosexuality

What the church teaches about homosexual conduct is brief and clear. The purpose of the sexual faculty is the expression of married love and the generation of new life in the context of the family. God calls us to use our faculties for the purposes for which they have been given to us. To use the sexual faculty in a way in which the generation of new life is impossible is to misuse it and is wrong. Genital sexual behavior between two persons of the same sex is such a misuse and is therefore wrong.

But this is not all that needs to be said. Other matters need careful attention by believers. One is an important distinction that needs to be made at the very outset of any discussion about homosexuality: the distinction between homosexual *activity* and a homosexual *orientation*.

Orientation vs. Activity

A true homosexual orientation is a spontaneous inclination or physical attraction to persons of the same sex. It is a person's principal and permanent sexual orientation. Nobody seems to know how or why such a homosexual orientation occurs. Is it hereditary? Induced? Acquired? We simply don't know for sure. But when such orientation occurs outside the conscious will of the homosexually oriented person, it is not a matter of personal guilt. It is something that happens to people, just as people happen to have other nondeliberate qualities such as an inclination to anger or a proclivity to avarice.

Homosexual orientation entails no more sin than short-ness or tallness. Is such an orientation a good thing in it-self? No, objectively speaking, it is a deficiency, a defect, but not a sin.

Homosexual activity, on the other hand, means engaging in genital sexual activity with persons of the same sex. Deliberate homosexual activity is wrong because it misuses the sexual faculty and is a sin to the extent that it is done knowingly and freely.

In our popular culture we often fail to distinguish be-tween orientation and behavior. We speak as if all homo-sexuals were sexually active, as if all homosexuals were compulsive persons who cannot (or do not) control their behavior, as if the inclination itself were culpable. This is an injustice on two counts: first, because people cannot be guilty of something for which they are not responsible (the orienta-tion); second, because indiscriminate sexual behavior is not characteristic of all homosexual persons.

Here is the fundamental Christian truth that must be re-spected in dealing with this issue: Homosexual persons enjoy the same human worth as everyone else. Their humanity has a claim to the same reverence and respect as the humanity of everyone else. Their existence is as much a sign of God's love as every other person's existence. Homosexual orientation does not cause persons to forfeit God's love. Neither does homosexual activity—or any sinful behavior, for that mat-ter—since God offers loving forgiveness of all sin to all of us.

Rights and Responsibilities

In view of every homosexual person's basic human worth, the church clearly teaches that homosexuals have rights. Violence, hatred or rejection directed toward homosexual persons is wrong. So is the refusal to provide housing or employment to someone exclusively on the grounds of that person's sexual orientation.

The church also teaches that the Christian community cannot ignore homosexual persons. The church's ministry is supposed to be as wide as God's love, a love that excludes no one. If there is any refuge to which the homosexual person ought to bring hurt and confusion and, of course, sin, it is to the church. If there is any context in which the homosexual person ought to feel comfortable in acknowledging the realities of his or her life, it ought to be in the church. The church indeed calls the homosexual person to chastity, but the church calls all members to the practice of chastity appropriate to their lives. The church indeed calls the active homosexual to repent for the sinfulness in his or her life, but the church calls all of us to repentance for our sins—and sexual sins are not necessarily the worst.

Yet, homosexuality remains a tough issue. This is not because church teaching is unclear or hard to understand, but because many reject the principles on which the teaching rests.

Points of Discord

Some are convinced that the church's moral argument from nature, that is, from the natural purpose of our sexual faculties, is invalid. To argue from presumed insights into the law of nature, they say, is excessively narrow and limits human variety and creativity. The church responds that any consistent approach to human nature must imply notions of what is compatible with human nature and what is not. Otherwise the very idea of "humanity" becomes meaningless.

Others hold that being requires expression in doing, that to refrain from genital expression of one's sexual orientation does violence to the human person, that people cannot discover themselves or realize their full potential unless they act upon their own sexuality, whatever its orientation. But this implies that persons who, for whatever reason, do not engage in genital sexual activity are not fully human. Most people find that suggestion unacceptable.

Apart from the critics who disagree about the basic principles, still other matters make homosexuality a tough issue.

The real violence and injustices inflicted on homosexual

persons prompt some to demand legal recognition for all homosexual behavior and a guarantee by society that the full homosexual lifestyle will be accepted on a par with traditional family life. Those who oppose this stance find themselves suspected of wanting to deny basic human rights to homosexuals.

Within the church some who feel that the church's ministry to homosexuals has not been sufficiently sensitive are now calling for a kind of acceptance of homosexual behavior which amounts to a complete about-face in the church's teaching. When church authorities oppose such a tendency, they are portrayed as pastorally harsh.

In addition, our culture allows very few ways in which honest and healthy affection can be expressed between persons of the same sex. Some individuals have a terror of homosexuality which results in an irrational phobia of everything remotely resembling it. Most recently, homosexually active persons have been identified as more likely than others to contract AIDS.

The sum of all this makes for a tough issue indeed. But in the midst of it all, some basic principles remain sure:

- Our human nature is not our own to do with as we please. It is a gift and, in using the gift, we must respect the giver.

- Human dignity belongs to all human beings. No form of behavior justifies despising another, still less any orientation or tendency for which the other is not even responsible.

- Participation in the community of the church does not depend on any perceived or real merit or excellence on the part of the believer. The church owes the compassion and the forgiveness of Christ to all of its members, including homosexual persons as well as those who would reject them. This is not watering down church teaching. It is a matter of being consistent in our efforts to offer to all who would receive it the embrace of a loving God.

Discussion Questions

1. What is my attitude toward homosexual persons?

2. How should families treat homosexual members?

3. What provision should civil law make in regard to homosexual persons?

For Further Reading

Catechism of the Catholic Church, 2357-2359.

Congregation for the Doctrine of the Faith, *Letter to the
Bishops of the Catholic Church on the Pastoral Care of
Homosexual Persons*, 1986 (*Origins* 16:22).

National Conference of Catholic Bishops Committee on
Marriage and the Family, *Always Our Children, a Pastoral
Message to Parents of Homosexual Children*, 1997 (*Origins*
27:17).

CHAPTER EIGHT

Social Justice

M any people find it hard to understand *why* the church should teach about economic systems, international debt, poverty, employment and the like. Aren't these questions better left to experts? Besides, economic concerns generally have political overtones and the folk wisdom of our country holds that the church is supposed to stay out of politics. When the church claims the right to scrutinize these matters, is it going beyond its competence?

No. These issues are not merely economic or political issues but moral issues as well. And it is in their moral dimension that the church addresses them, even as the church addresses the moral dimension of warfare, of political responsibility and of many other things.

Why the Church Speaks Out

The basic insight of the church's social teaching is that social systems do not just happen. They result from human activity and human decisions. A society's treatment of its poor, for example, is not determined by an eternal decree imposed from above. Rather, the way a society treats its poor is determined by a whole series of small decisions and determinations that gradually find expression in custom and law, which, in turn, form part of the society's larger economic and political system. Things get the way they are because of human decisions.

More importantly, social systems can be changed. They

are not cast in bronze forever. What came from human decisions can be modified, or even eliminated, by human decisions. There was a time, for example, when health insurance was not available to anyone in our country. Now it is more widely available because human beings made and carried out decisions. Just a few decades ago, black persons in this country were economically and socially oppressed by law and custom. While racial injustice still persists, human decisions and choices have resulted in an improved system.

Economic and political systems can be unjust. For example, a system which allows only millionaires to own property or to participate in political life is wrong. A system in which women do the same work as men but are paid less is wrong. Maybe the people presently in charge of a social system, who wield the power, are not personally responsible for the system they inherited. They did not make it unjust. But, given that the system can be changed, they are the cause of the system remaining unjust if they refuse to change it. They have intellect and free will, and they are responsible for what they do and for what they fail to do.

Intellect and free will and responsibility and choice are the stuff of morality. The church's right to talk about the justice and injustice of social systems is the same as the church's right to talk about stealing and telling lies. In both contexts the church is dealing with human choices, and that constitutes morality.

This explains *why* the church teaches about economic matters. But because many people find economic matters themselves so complex, they conclude that the church's teaching must be equally complex. They hesitate to ask *what* the church teaches. Yet the foundation for the church's teaching about social justice consists of principles which are already familiar.

Basic Principles

Most fundamental is the principle of human dignity: All human beings have a right to a particular reverence and respect simply because they are creatures of a loving God. Just as the individual person must respect the dignity of all other human beings, so also an economic system must respect the dignity of all human beings. Any arrangement which enslaves human beings, causes them to live without hope, or uses them as disposable means for purposes beyond themselves is an immoral arrangement because it is in disaccord with the demands of human dignity.

Equally fundamental is the principle of the human community. Nobody lives all alone in the world and nobody can survive without interacting with others. Each of us must receive from others, and each of us must give to others. We depend on each other for food, clothing, protection and for many other things as well. Not one of us can be excluded from the human community; we all have the right and the responsibility to participate.

On the basis of these principles, the church teaches that every approach to social and political life that claims to be humane, moral and Christian must be shaped by three questions: What does the system do *for* people? What does it do *to* people? And how do people *participate*? The basic issue implicit in these questions is how human dignity is protected and promoted.

The ramifications of all this are far-reaching. These basic moral principles provide the yardstick to measure the morality of the way a society distributes wealth, the criteria it uses in the exercise of power, its attitudes toward the poor, the protection it provides to individuals and to families and a thousand other matters. The application of the principles is not always easy, and even people who agree about the principles can sometimes disagree about their application. But the principles are there, and they are moral principles.

Having considered *why* and *what* the church teaches on matters of social justice leaves still another area of difficulty. Granted that systems can be changed; granted that morality is involved in economic questions; what is my responsibility as a Christian believer in all this?

Today's issues are immensely complicated, and the inertia of any system which already exists is great. Change and development in an economic system require political and social

resources that are almost beyond comprehension, let alone individual influence. How can I, one person in a world of mil-
lions, respond to what the church teaches on these matters?
What is my responsibility?

Personal Response

Obviously I do not bear personal responsibility for the origin
of the injustices and inequities in our present economic system. Nor do I bear the responsibility to change the system
single-handedly. But I am responsible for dealing with injustice to the extent to which I am able. I am responsible for making my individual contribution to efforts and attitudes aimed
at protecting and promoting human dignity.

This means being aware of the realities. We can easily
close our eyes to the needs of those around us—and still more
easily overlook the needs of those far away.

It also means trying to use individual resources wisely
and justly and common resources fairly. Is my salary all for
me, or do I see that others have a claim on it too? What kind
of a consumer am I? Do I buy, use up and throw away everything which media advertising says I am supposed to buy, use
up and throw away?

My personal convictions constitute a major element in my
relationship with the society around me. Do I accept all the
prejudices of the system: "People are poor because they don't
want to work," "I am prosperous only because of my own efforts," "Only the wealthy have the right to power"? Or do I
test so-called common wisdom with Christian standards?
What issues do I take into account when I vote? Do I even
vote?

Some believers have the talents and opportunities to engage in economic or political activity on a wider, more public
scale. Catholic teaching invites them to see these possibilities
as a call to serve humanity in a special way. Being in business
or politics offers an opportunity to work for the dignity of humankind in a way that few others enjoy.

Social justice is a tough issue partly because it is so big.

Even if we are clear about why the church teaches about these matters, the scope and implications of the teaching are so vast that they are difficult to grasp. Moreover, we are tempted to see our individual efforts as insignificant. But the fact remains that our loving God is concerned about the economic and social structures in which we live, just as God is concerned about the actions and attitudes of all the individuals who determine, however remotely, what those structures are to be.

Discussion Questions

1. How do the social, economic and political structures of our country affect my life?

2. To what extent do I see myself responsible for what goes on in our country? How does this call me to action?

3. Do I see voting as a moral obligation? Why? Why not?

For Further Reading

Catechism of the Catholic Church, 2426–2449.

Pope John Paul II, Encyclical Letter *Centesimus Annus*, 1991 (*Origins* 21:1).

United States Catholic Conference Administrative Committee, *Faithful Citizenship*, 1999 (*Origins* 29:20).

CHAPTER NINE

Warfare

M ost people simply do not want to question the rightness of warfare. This issue can seem too difficult, too complicated, all the options apparently unsatisfactory. Whether it is the rightness of making war in general or the rightness of a specific war, the questioner can generally expect accusations of cowardice, lack of patriotism or childish idealism.

There are several typical ways in which people think about war:

First, some think all warfare is wrong. Their position finds simply no justification, at any time or in any circumstance, for opposing another human being to the extent of taking that human being's life, even in order to defend one's own. The evils arising from waging war are always judged greater than the evils from not waging war.

A second approach sees warfare as a dirty business which is sometimes inevitable. It concludes that the best war is the quickest war, no matter what it may entail.

The Catholic Christian tradition offers a third approach to the question of warfare. Church tradition teaches that because warfare is a matter of human freedom (human decisions and human choices), it is a moral question. There are circumstances in which war can be justified, just as there are circumstances in which war cannot be justified. The decision about the justification of warfare is based on criteria ultimately concerned with the basic principles of human dignity and of respect for human life. These two principles, taken together, offer the basis for what is known as the just war teaching.

Traditional Moral Criteria

The church's just war teaching says that defense of innocent victims against unjust aggression is legitimate and moral. We are not obliged to accept every injustice, every injury that others would inflict on us. Society is allowed to defend itself against organized aggression from without, just as society is allowed to defend itself from the aggression of individuals from within. Yet we must do our best to prevent our defense from degenerating into unjust aggression. The presumption, based on human experience, is that it will. For that reason, the just war teaching offers guidelines which help us decide when engaging in war as self-defense is moral. These guidelines include:

- The cause must be just. A clear and present danger must threaten the conditions necessary to preserve decent human existence and basic human rights.

- The common good must be at issue, not just the well-being of private groups or individuals. Similarly, war must always be authorized by a competent authority, although sometimes the competent authority may be the people whose natural human dignity and rights are being oppressed by an unjust government.

- Those who would justly wage war must have a predominance of justice on their side. Rarely, if ever, is all the right on one side and all the wrong on another. Those who would wage war justly must be convinced that the rights they are defending are greater than the rights which the aggressors claim to assert.

- War must be waged with a right intention, an intention to settle the injustice and no more.

- War must be a last resort. All peaceful alternatives must have been tried and exhausted.

- There must be a probability of success. If there is absolutely no hope of settling the injustice, there is no moral justification for entering the conflict.

- The rights to be defended must be proportionate to the damage that necessarily accompanies entry into warfare. What we are fighting for must be worth the price that will necessarily be paid even by those who win.

Traditional Christian teaching presents these criteria for determining whether *entering* a war is moral. Other criteria must be observed if *carrying on* the war is to be moral. These are the criteria of proportionality and discrimination.

What we do in the course of the war must be proportionate to the rights we are trying to defend. Not everything which is done in the pursuit of justice is automatically moral. To inflict injustice in order to defend justice is never right.

Finally, we must discriminate between those who are in the war and those who are not. To attack noncombatants or nonmilitary targets just because they are attached to a people with whom we happen to be at war is not moral.

Modern Complexities

But to have enunciated the basic points of the just war teaching is not yet to have answered all the questions. In a world which is increasingly interdependent and in which the behavior of one country affects all the others, who has the right to declare war, even a just war? What alternatives must first be exhausted? How can the principle of proportionality be observed, either in entering or in prosecuting a war, if the weapons employed necessarily entail general destruction and the effective ruin of all those who use them, whether winners or losers? Can using such weapons ever be in accord with the demands of a just war? If the use of such weapons, or some uses of them, is immoral, is *threatening* to use them permissible in order to maintain peace? How can one discriminate between combatants and noncombatants when whole societies somehow contribute to the war effort and when the destruction which is threatened or executed cannot be limited to care-fully defined targets?

Some say that the traditional just war teaching is outdated due to the realities of nuclear warfare. This does not seem to be exact. The traditional just war teaching is as valid and as useful as ever in determining when war is just, but its criteria lead many to conclude that warfare in the nuclear age is far more difficult to justify than were wars in other times, if indeed it is not completely beyond justification.

Yet the question of warfare is a moral question and the immensity of the problems inherent in modern warfare does not excuse us from exercising moral criteria in evaluating those problems. We cannot leave judgment about such matters to soldiers and leaders alone, because the human dignity at issue is ours. We all share responsibility for how our human dignity is treated. To refuse to think in moral categories about war is to surrender ahead of time to barbarism and injustice.

To Serve or Not to Serve?

Two other matters call for comment. One is the role of the Christian believer in military service. The other is the question of pacifism and nonviolence.

Full-scale modern warfare is hard to justify. But the purpose of a country's military forces is, in large part, to make war unnecessary. The capacity to defend one's rights reduces the probability that those rights will be attacked. Thus, the women and men of the military contribute to the peace and the security of their fellow citizens. For that they deserve our gratitude.

From the earliest times in the church, however, there have been persons conscientiously convinced that killing or violence even in the defense of right and justice can never be justified, that such behavior is more destructive to human dignity in the long run than the violation of rights by an aggressor. The church teaches that this position can be morally held by an individual and calls for appropriate provision to be made in law for those who conscientiously object to all warfare or even to a specific war.

These persons are not stupid or cowardly, but brave women and men who keep alive the moral sensitivities of the rest of us. Even when we have weighed the conflict between justice and aggression as carefully as we can, even when we have made the reluctant moral decision that armed resistance is appropriate, this troublesome witness to another position (that is, pacifism or nonviolence) demands that we continue to consider whether the decision we have made is the only one, or a right one, or a good one. Given the complexities we deal with even in matters of self-defense, we continue to need this witness.

Warfare is a tough issue, so tough that we do not even like to think about it. Yet think about it we must. Our culture would have us see war as a necessary—and occasionally glorious—endeavor whose demands take precedence over every other consideration. Folk wisdom says, "All's fair in love and war." But the God who loves us human creatures says, "No, it isn't."

Discussion Questions

1. What have been my first- and second-hand experiences of war?

2. Which of our country's wars have been just in their origin and in their execution?

3. Why does a country tend to treat severely those who question the legitimacy of its wars?

For Further Reading

Catechism of the Catholic Church, 2307–2317.

Vatican Council II, *Pastoral Constitution on the Church in the Modern World*, 1965, nos. 79–82.

National Conference of Catholic Bishops, Pastoral Letter *The Challenge of Peace*, 1983 (*Origins* 13:1).

CHAPTER TEN

Church Membership

Does it really matter which church I belong to? Does God care? Most people in our society would answer no to both these questions. The common wisdom in the United States is that religious affiliation is a totally private matter. It is also a matter of personal taste and personal choice. Just as there is no "right" choice between chardonnay or merlot, so also there is no one "right" choice when it comes to determining what church to join. Wherever you feel most comfortable is where you belong.

In addition to those basic attitudes, which speak to an individual's personal decisions, there is also our public stance toward religion. People speak with great reverence about our American "wall of separation" between church and state. The provision of the first amendment to our Constitution which forbids Congress from setting up an "established" religion for our country is interpreted to mean that civil government may not show any interest in the religious community. Government has to act as if religion does not exist. For any individual or group to contend that its religious community puts forward claims that other religious communities cannot advance is not only ill-mannered but unpatriotic as well.

Well-informed Catholics do not agree with such a posture toward religion. They believe that their Catholic faith has elements that other religious faiths do not and cannot claim to have and that, all things being equal, it would be sinful for someone to refuse, freely and deliberately, to become a member of the Catholic church. This stance puts us out of harmony with most of our fellow citizens. That's why, for Catholics at least, church membership is a tough issue.

In order to appreciate what Catholics believe on this matter, it is important to be clear about what Catholics believe about the nature of the church and about the response to the church that God calls for from us.

What the Church Is

Catholics believe that Jesus is both human and divine and that in Jesus God came to earth as a human being to bring us back into union with God through the faithfulness and self-sacrifice that he expressed during his earthly life. Catholics believe that Jesus died and rose from the dead and is, therefore, still alive. We believe that Jesus extends to those who give themselves to him a participation in his risen life. This is what constitutes salvation.

Because all those who accept Jesus'offer of life in himself share the one life of the risen Christ, they constitute one single community, a community of faith. This we call the church. We believe it is a community willed and founded by Christ.

Because Christ intended this community of faith to spread throughout the world and persist over all the ages, he provided it with a visible structure. It is not just some sort of invisible "state of mind." He also provided it with other elements of life and holiness: seven sacraments, inspired Scriptures, a teaching authority, the encouragement that comes from the good example of other brothers and sisters in the faith. All these elements are part of what Christ meant his one community of faith to enjoy.

There are many Christian communities that claim to be the church that Christ founded. They vary in their modes of governance, in the relative emphasis they give to the sacraments and sacred Scripture, in the particularities of their historical development. Catholics believe that certain elements of salvation can be found in these Christian church communities. But Catholics also believe that the full spectrum of elements of salvation that Christ wanted his community of faith to enjoy is found only in the Catholic church and that, therefore, the Catholic church is the church Christ founded.

Belonging and Not Belonging

Catholics believe that Christ calls us all to share his risen life, that this risen life comes to us through the elements of salvation that Christ entrusted to his church, and that the church Christ founded is the Catholic church. It follows that, if we want to share fully in the risen life of Christ (a sharing that constitutes our salvation) we have to belong to the Catholic church. To turn away freely and deliberately from the salvation that Christ offers us in his church constitutes the rejection of salvation. We cannot be saved if we freely and deliberately refuse to accept the salvation that Christ offers us.

Does that mean that all those who are outside the Catholic church cannot be saved? No, it does not. The church teaches us that, although the fullness of the means of salvation can be found only in the Catholic church, the elements of salvation that exist in other Christian church communities (for example, baptism and the Bible) do not lose their efficacy. To the extent that members of these other Christian communities accept the gifts that God offers, they, too, can be saved.

Similarly, even those who have never heard the gospel of Christ or have not even arrived at an explicit knowledge of God can be saved if they strive to do what is right according to their lights. Their salvation comes from Christ and consists in the sharing of Christ's life even though they are not aware of him. The reason is not that formal and explicit Christian faith is not important, but that there is no salvation without Christ and that those who extend themselves toward goodness as they know it are implicitly reaching out toward Christ.

Getting It Right

What the church teaches about the necessity of belonging to the church that Christ founded is a tough issue because it is open to such misinterpretation, confusion and exaggeration on the part of Catholics and non-Catholics alike.

It is not the case that Catholics think they are better than everybody else. Catholics know their faith is a freely given gift from God. Personal worth has nothing to do with God's giving the gift and nothing to do with God's preservation of it once it has been given. In fact, if Catholics think that their membership in the church is a result of their own spiritual achievement, they are not being faithful to the church's teaching.

It is not the case that Catholics think that everybody who is not Catholic is going to end up in hell. The church teaches clearly that salvation is available to all human beings, provided only that they do what they know is right and remain open to God's gifts.

It is not the case that Catholics would really like to establish Catholicism as an "official" religion and then make everybody join the Catholic church. We have learned over the ages that only a freely accepted and voluntarily practiced faith keeps us in touch with the risen life of Christ.

Religious affiliation is not a matter of pure personal preference. That might be the case if religions or varieties of religious faith were all products of human ingenuity. Then it would not matter if we chose one affiliation over another, because they would all be ultimately the same: man-made articles of more or less equal worth. But that's not how it is. God has something to say about how he wants to be worshipped and he has said it through the life, death and resurrection of Jesus. God continues to address us and care for us through the church that Jesus founded.

Discussion Questions

1. How do I regard the religious faith of my friends who are not Catholic?

2. If I am not free to "shop around" among varieties of Christian churches, is it acceptable to "shop around" among various varieties and tonalities of Catholic parishes? Why? Why not?

3. Is it permissible for Catholics to pray for a non-Catholic or non-Christian who has died? Why? Why not?

For Further Reading

Vatican Council II, *Dogmatic Constitution on the Church*, nos. 1–17.

Congregation for the Doctrine of the Faith, *Declaration on the Unicity and Salvific Universality of Jesus Christ and the Church*, 2000 (*Origins* 30:14).

CHAPTER ELEVEN

Priestly Celibacy

Is the church right to insist that priests be celibate? Before we answer that question, some clarification is called for.

Priestly celibacy is a law, a regulation, not revealed truth or a "rule" derived from basic moral principles. Nothing in the teaching of Jesus requires that all those who serve the church in the ordained ministry of priesthood remain unmarried. In fact, at some periods of the church's history, only those priests who were vowed religious were celibate. Even today in some areas of the church (mostly in the Middle East), Catholic priests are husbands and fathers of families. Nonetheless, where the law of priestly celibacy is in force, it has a teaching or witnessing purpose. It says something about the church and about priestly ministry.

Celibacy as Witness

What does priestly celibacy say?

For one thing, priestly celibacy reflects the teaching of Jesus about the urgency of the kingdom of God. Jesus taught that nothing is more important than God's love and God's action in our midst. Even the deepest human associations are secondary to the demands of God's love. The celibacy of priests is witness to this teaching. It is not a matter of marriage being bad or a second-rate vocation.

It is rather a matter of perspective, of relativity. The celibacy of priests is a constant reminder to God's people that, in the final analysis, there are some things which take precedence over others, good as those other things might be.

The celibacy of priests is also a sign of God's love for the community of the church. The presence among God's people of a whole category of persons whose central purpose in life is to care for the Christian community as ordained leaders is a reflection of the unswerving love and attention which God provides to those who believe in him.

Finally, the celibacy of the priest is intended to be a symbol of the eternal future to which God calls us, a future in which all human relationships, even the most sacred and most fulfilling, will be secondary to the loving union between ourselves and the Lord. The celibate priest is supposed to signify to God's people here and now that future state.

Given its fundamental teaching and witnessing function, priestly celibacy can only be understood in the context of the church as a whole. The celibate priesthood only makes sense as part of the church community, not off by itself. It is not the case that it is always better to be a priest than to be married. Nor have those who have married opted for something less perfect for themselves. It is rather, that those special emphases of which the church needs to be reminded seem to be best provided if its ordained priestly ministers are also signs and symbols of realities such as the urgency of the kingdom, of the intensity of God's love for the church and the future state of complete union between ourselves and God.

Questions about Celibacy

But other facets of the question expose the toughness of the issue.

In many places priests are too few to provide the sacraments for the people in a regular way. In our own country, as the number of priests declines, we will need to become accustomed to a new way of being church. Wouldn't it be better to ordain married men to care for God's people?

Moreover, since married life is as much a sacred vocation as priesthood, wouldn't it be appropriate to have married priests witness to the sanctity of marriage? Wouldn't married priests understand the realities of married life better than celibates?

Again, if celibacy is unattractive to prospective priests these days, should church leaders not acknowledge that this church law is inappropriate to our culture and our time?

Given that some priests find the demands of priestly ministry more than they can bear alone, shouldn't they be allowed to enter marriage and continue their priestly ministry?

For that matter, why should the church not permit both celibate and married priests in the local church community, each giving witness in their way to the various realities of Christian life?

These questions are not impertinent or disloyal. But neither are they the only questions. If the present requirement of priestly celibacy is a teaching instrument for the church, what teaching would be implied in a change of the church's law? Apart from the teaching or witnessing component, what other consequences would result from such a change?

Implications of a Change

If prospective candidates are less numerous today because they have been persuaded that genital sexuality is essential to human fulfillment, would not a change in the requirement of priestly celibacy seem to indicate that the church has finally bought into this presumption?

What would be the relationship between the priest's ministry and his marriage? The theology and spirituality of Catholic priesthood has seen the priestly vocation as a full-time, lifetime, totally dedicated lifestyle in which the priest gives himself exclusively to his ministry. Likewise, the Catholic theology of marriage has seen the married state as the prime dedication of the spouses to one another and to their family, a dedication to which every other human relationship must take second place.

If married men were ordained to priesthood, would the conclusion be that the church no longer sees priestly ministry as it did before, or would the conclusion be that marriage means something different to the priest, who gives to his family as much time and dedication as he can spare from his priestly ministry? And if the priest's marriage is seen in this subsidiary way, what about the marriage of other believers?

If some priests really find the responsibilities of their ministry too heavy to bear alone, what would the additional responsibilities of wife and family do to them?

As regards the shortage question, how do we know that ordaining married men would be an adequate response? The suggestion assumes that the numbers of celibate priests would remain constant and that enough married men would come forward to make up the required difference. Could not the number of potential celibate priests decrease, since such persons would be asking themselves why they should make a full-time, celibate gift of their lives to the church when the church no longer seems to value such a gift? Moreover, expecting the same total service from a married priest which we now expect from celibate priests would be unrealistic, and so greater numbers of married priests would be required to carry out the same level of ministry we now have. To say that such numbers would surely be forthcoming is an unproved assertion.

A Judgment Call

We have here pros and cons, from which still further pros and cons arise. Whatever is said on the issue of priestly celibacy always seems to leave room for at least one more "Yes, but..." It is not a simple issue in which "optional celibacy" is the clear and universal solution.

The church's law of celibacy for priests is essentially a judgment call. As the question has been considered again and again over the centuries, church leadership has consistently decided that a celibate priesthood is best for the church's mission at large.

The church's law of priestly celibacy says that, on balance, the people of God are best served by having a distinct group of official leaders in ministry who, by the basic circumstances of their life, give witness to the overriding demands of God's kingdom, to God's undivided concern for the church, and to a way of life still to come in which the whole meaning of our existence will be expressed in our relationship with God.

The church sees the celibacy of its priests as a gift—a gift *from God* who equips and chooses persons for a particular role in the church and a gift *from those who answer the call* of God and the church. The gift is not always easy to accept or to give. The gift can be misused, misunderstood, undervalued and questioned. But in the last analysis it is a gift that speaks of God's love for the community of the church.

Discussion Questions

1. How is the celibacy of the priests who serve me a gift to the church and to me?

2. Have I ever considered dedicating my life to the service of the church? Have I ever encouraged anybody else to do so?

3. Is there any difference between being celibate and being unmarried?

For Further Reading

Catechism of the Catholic Church, 1579–1580.

Vatican Council II, *Decree on the Ministry and Life of Priests*, 1965, no. 16.

National Conference of Catholic Bishops, Committee on Vocations, *Statement on Vocations to the Priesthood*, 1989 (*Origins* 19:22).

CHAPTER TWELVE

Ordination of Women

I sn't it unjust of the church to refuse women ordination to the priesthood? Isn't it time to lift this ban?

On this issue, as on all others, knowing exactly what is in question is crucial. Here we are not talking about a law or a rule, but about a teaching. The church has not decided that women ought not be ordained to priesthood, but teaches that women cannot be ordained to priesthood—that is, that it is not possible for a woman to be an ordained priest.

This teaching has not been formally and dogmatically defined like the divinity of Christ. But it is not an open question in which all opinions are equally valid. Perhaps the best way to reach an understanding of the church's teaching is to consider some of the elements inherent in it.

Historical Precedent and Sacramental Substance

Central to the church's teaching is historical precedent. No evidence indicates that women have ever been ordained to priesthood throughout the church's long history. Is this a historical accident? Is the church's practice culturally determined and therefore open to change as human culture changes? Or does the church's practice reflect the normative will of Christ?

Because ordination is a sacrament, the origin and nature of the seven sacraments are also at issue here. The church believes that the sacraments have their origin in Christ, that he instituted them. If this is the case, to what extent is the church able to modify sacramental practice?

While the church can determine, for example, that lay persons may distribute the Eucharist, the church cannot determine that the matter of the Eucharist can be rice and tea rather than bread and wine. Similarly, the church can determine that Christian marriage vows must be exchanged in the presence of a priest and two witnesses, rather than by the parties alone, but the church cannot decide that a sacramental marriage can be contracted between persons still bound by another marriage.

Here, then, is the real issue: Is the practice of not ordaining women one of those things which the church can change, or is it something which is inherent in the substance of the sacrament of orders and therefore not subject to church determination? The consensus of the church has always been that this is not something open to change.

Having said that, we then find ourselves asking why the church cannot change the substance of the sacraments to correspond more closely to the perceived needs and customs of today. The reason is that the sacraments are a reflection of Jesus'own historical life and ministry.

Christian faith and ritual practice are founded in the events of the life of a man who lived and taught in the cultural context of first-century Palestine. This is why we use bread and wine, instead of rice and tea, to recall Christ's last supper with his apostles. This is why we use oil, instead of iodine, to express Christ's healing and strengthening of the sick. And this is why priests, who represent the historical Jesus in a particular way, are male and not female. The church is not free to change the substance of the sacraments because the sacraments reflect the historical reality of Jesus, and the church cannot change that reality.

Further Questions

Still further questions need to be dealt with if we want to understand the church's teaching on this issue.

What does it mean to be a priest in the church? Is the ordained priesthood some sort of elite class to which all others are subordinate and which women are unworthy to enter? Or is the priesthood a particular service to the church to which some are called for the good of the church? Because some are called to priesthood are others less worthy, less good? Does the fact that almost all members of the church are not priests mean that priesthood is something which only a few deserve, or does it mean that baptism provides the basic mode of being Christian and that the ordained priesthood exists only to promote and serve the well-being of the general body of believers?

Then there is the question of power in the church. Priests have certain powers that other church members do not. Does this mean that only priests are important in the church? What is the nature of "power" in the church? Is there only one kind?

The contemporary phenomenon of the expansion of church ministry adds another dimension to the discussion. Not too long ago, church ministry was reserved almost exclusively to the priest. He did everything, and did it almost alone. Now religious sisters and brothers and lay men and women engage in service to the church community as catechists, youth ministers, visitors of the sick, directors of catechumenates and so on. Does the desire of some women to be ordained to priesthood reflect progress or regression in the direction of restricting all real ministry to priesthood?

But what about the Protestant communities which have women ministers? Here we must recall that most Protestant churches do not look on holy orders as a sacrament. They see their minister as a member of the congregation called and deputed for service by the congregation itself without any special sacramental action from God.

Not an Arbitrary Decision

There are all sorts of questions which arise as we try to understand the church's teaching about the ordination of women. That's what makes it a tough issue. But it is important to acknowledge that we are not dealing here with some arbitrary decision on the part of sexist church leaders who could easily do things differently if they chose. Rather we are dealing with the church's conscientious attempt to be faithful to the teaching and will of Christ.

Still other things need to be said. The church's teaching about who is able to receive the sacrament of holy orders is not a sign that women—or unordained men, for that matter—are somehow inferior in the church. When we talk about priesthood, we are not talking about "superior" and "inferior" but about "different." The ministry of ordained priesthood is the Lord expressing his love for us in one way. The care and service offered to the church and the world by dedicated lay women and men is another. Both are gifts. We cannot afford to undervalue either.

Therefore, excluding women from church activities which they are able and permitted to do is wrong. This includes various service ministries and many liturgical ministries as well. Increased visibility and participation of women has been one of the church's greatest blessings in the last few decades. Unfortunately, some of the church's representatives have not always been as diligent as they might have been in encouraging and promoting greater participation of women. Some church members have resisted accepting women's activity in new roles within the community. This, too, is unfortunate.

Many find it hard to see the handiwork of a loving God in the church's teaching about women's ordination; many find it a difficult and painful issue; but the fact that this teaching is hard for some to understand, or hard for some to accept, does not make it wrong or mean that it should be rejected. Christ loves his church and guides it and blesses it in many ways. Our task, in the midst of the pain and difficulty of faithfulness, is to search for the insights and understandings that will make clear where the blessings lie.

Discussion Questions

1. What ministerial roles do women exercise in my parish? When did they begin to do so?

2. Why is it important to stress that baptism, not ordination, provides the basic mode of being Christian?

3. In what ways do I see priesthood as a ministry of service rather than a mechanism of control?

For Further Reading

Catechism of the Catholic Church, 1577–1578.

Pope John Paul II, Apostolic Letter *Muleris Dignitatem*, 1988, nos. 26–27. (*Origins* 18:17).

National Conference of Catholic Bishops, Committee on Doctrine, *Ten Frequently Asked Questions About the Reservation of Priestly Ordination to Men*, 1998 (*Origins* 28:20).

CHAPTER THIRTEEN

Authority in the Church

We all have had problems with authority at some time in our lives. Maybe the problems were the result of our immaturity, as when we simply could not understand why touching a hot stove would be such a bad thing. Maybe our problems were the result of what seemed to be injustice or ineptitude on the part of those who exercised authority, as when the police seemed interested in speeders only when we were going too fast.

Authority will always be a source of problems unless we have a correct idea of its nature and purpose. The dictionary defines authority as "the power to require and receive submission or assent; the right to expect obedience; the right to command." But there is more to it than compulsion. The Latin root from which our English word is derived has overtones of originating something, of making something grow. It suggests empowerment or enablement.

Instinctively we know that both good authority and bad authority exist. To be good, authority must, first of all, have a legitimate origin. That is, the person charged with authority must derive the authority from an appropriate source. Thus, the police chief's authority is good because it is given by the community. The authority of the Mafia leader is bad because it is taken by violence.

In addition to legitimate origin, authority must be properly exercised. Even the chief of police can cause problems if he or she exercises authority in an arbitrary fashion. Authority does not have to be authoritarian.

What is authority's purpose? Ultimately all authority has a community purpose—to do something in and for a group of people. In civil society, authority exists to protect citizens from crime, to see that the laws are carried out and to arbitrate disputed rights. In other words, civil authority makes it possible for citizens to pursue the well-being for which society exists. In an army, authority exists to coordinate soldiers so that they can carry out the purpose for which the army exists.

All authority exists in order to keep a community or a group in touch with its purpose. Authority preserves and fosters the goal and the activity of the community or group. It removes obstacles, provides opportunities, encourages, defends, restrains, empowers. Authority makes it possible, in various social contexts, for us to do what we are supposed to do and be what we are supposed to be. Far from being a burden to which we must submit, authority is an instrument of liberation. Authority enables us to be free in the context of community.

For the Sake of Mission

The church's purpose is to continue the mission of Christ. Jesus could not be present always and everywhere in the same way he was present in Palestine. But God wanted all future generations to receive the offer of salvation in Christ. So God gave us the church. In order to carry out its purpose, the church has authority.

The church does what Christ did with his same authority both in the world and within the community of believers.

Just as Jesus in his time taught the world about his father's love and called women and men to sanctity, so also the church in every age and place teaches and sanctifies and calls human beings to respond to its teaching and its promise of holiness; and it does all this with Christ's authority.

The church does not present itself to the world as some kind of voluntary organization to which some people find it pleasant to belong. On the contrary, the church presents itself to the world as the authorized representative of the Son of God, as the community of believers which has the power and the responsibility to speak and act for its Lord, as the agent of the one in whom alone humankind finds its meaning and salvation. The church stands before the world with authority because Christ stood before the world with authority.

Obviously, the church must be faithful to the authority it has received from Christ, and it cannot make claims for itself beyond that authorization. What is offered as his teaching and his sanctifying power must in fact be from him. In carrying out its mission to the world, the church's authority is not autocratic or limitless, but is subject to Christ, to his action, to his Word.

The church has to have authority in order to be an effective extension of the life and teaching of Christ. The church cannot adequately represent Christ unless it is able to make the same claims on those being addressed today as he himself made on those whom he taught and healed and sanctified.

For the Sake of Identity

Just as the church enjoys authority in reaching out to the world to continue its mission, so also the church enjoys authority in its interior life in order to remain in touch with its own identity. Authority within the church exists in order to enable God's people to be what God wants them to be. And just as the church's authority over the proclamation of the gospel to the world must remain subject and faithful to the reality of Christ, so also authority within the church community is subject and faithful to Christ.

There are all kinds of authority within the church: the authority of religious superiors toward their sisters and brothers; the authority of parents toward their children (an authority which is something more for Christian believers than the natural dominance of mother and father over offspring); the authority of spouses toward one another as they express in their married life the relationship of Christ to his people; the authority of the saints, who by their lives illustrate and communicate the Lord's call to holiness; the authority of the priest in the sacrament of reconciliation, who tells us what we must do in order to have our sins forgiven and stay clear of them in the future; the authority of the pastor who bears the responsibility of fostering a local community of believers in that part of the diocese which constitutes his parish.

Some bear authority in the context of the whole church. These are the pope and the bishops in union with him. Their authority has to do with the universal teaching of the church and with the church's universal well-being. They bear the responsibility for the preservation and communication of Christ's teaching; for the availability of the means of holiness which Christ gave his church; for the general organizational well-being of the whole people of God.

Because they have these responsibilities, church leaders have a corresponding authority. In the exercise of this authority, church leaders will always be concerned about reverent preservation, about weeding out everything foreign to the mission and teaching of Christ. But they will also be concerned about searching out new ways of proclaiming and carrying out the will of the Lord in the ever-changing context of human reality.

Authority within the church has many forms, but the purpose of each is the same: to enable the church to remain in touch with its Lord, to help God's people remain faithful to their Lord.

Authority is one of the basic ways in which the church looks after its identity, in which the church safeguards its faithfulness to Christ. Authority in the church empowers us to be consistent with what God has made us to be; it protects us from error and self-destruction; it sets us free.

Authority in the church can be a tough issue if we treat it as something oppressive and distasteful. But if we recognize its purpose, we will be able to find within it a major gift of the God who so loves us human creatures.

Discussion Questions

1. Have I experienced church authority as a blessing or as a burden?

2. What would happen if there were no authority in the church?

3. Is there any sense in which it is correct to say that every member shares in the authority of the church?

For Further Reading

Catechism of the Catholic Church, 871–913.

Pope John Paul II, Encyclical Letter *Veritatis Splendor,* 1993, nos. 84–106 (*Origins* 23:18).

CHAPTER FOURTEEN

Conscience

We know our conscience must guide us when difficult decisions are to be made. We speak of doing things in "good conscience" or "bad conscience." We say, "My conscience is clear," or, "My conscience is bothering me." We talk about freedom of conscience. We refer to a good person as conscientious and to bad conduct as unconscionable.

But what is *conscience*?

Basically, conscience is the power of making a judgment between good and evil. The judgment has to do with how moral principles and values apply to a concrete situation. Conscience answers the question: "What is the right thing for me to do here and now?"

An appropriate answer depends upon three elements: knowledge, evaluation and application.

First, we must know what is right in general. We need to have assimilated from family, neighbors, school and church the general demands of goodness, of moral behavior. We have to know what the moral "rules" are, rules which are rooted in teachings about God and humanity, about good and bad.

Second, we need to evaluate the specific circumstances in which we find ourselves. Which circumstances in a situation are important and which are not? Which are of primary importance and which are secondary?

Third, we need to apply the moral principles and values to our specific circumstances. This implies discerning the fit between our circumstances, as we have analyzed them, and the moral principles and values according to which we direct our lives.

Conscience, then, deals with moral principles and values, with specific circumstances and with the linkage between them.

Because we are individual spiritual beings gifted with intellect and will, each faced with our own personal mix of situations and circumstances, we cannot avoid making personal judgments of conscience. We cannot turn all moral decision making over to someone else. We are called to do right, and we are responsible for what we do. The discernment of what is right here and now, for which we are individually answerable, is the work of conscience.

Following Conscience

Our conscience is the final norm for judging the morality of our action, here in our life, now. Nothing, no one else can take its place. This is what it means to be guided by our conscience.

Does this mean that I must follow my conscience even if my conscience is mistaken? Yes, but I am not therefore allowed to do anything I want on the plea that I am following my conscience. Nor may I neglect learning what is right in order to have a conscience that is easier to live with. I have an obligation to follow my conscience, but I also have an equal obligation to *form* my conscience, to do what is necessary for its proper functioning.

Forming Conscience

To accomplish that, we first need instruction. We need to understand where our life comes from, what its purpose is, how we are to reach the goal set for us beyond ourselves and beyond the whims of the moment, what is important and what is illusionary. For this instruction we turn to the word of God and the teachings of the church.

God's love gives us guidance through the teaching of the church. The community of the faithful has not only received the word of God, but also has prayed over it, reflected on it and tried to live it through the ages.

The moral teaching of the church looks on reality not in terms of individual preferences here and now, but in terms of how the love of God is to be expressed in the life of all the faithful. The formation of our consciences, the assimilation of the church's moral teaching, is one of the most important tasks we face in life. What we do determines what we become, and in order to do what is right, we first have to *know* what is right.

In this context it seems appropriate to repeat something said in the introduction to this book: Doing what is wrong is always harmful; doing what is good is beneficial. Goodness corresponds to reality, to the way in which God created us to live.

If I do wrong, I fly in the face of reality, I inflict injury on myself or others. If I am ignorant of right and wrong, I will make wrong moral judgments about what I am called upon to do. I may be subjectively free of fault because I am following my conscience, erroneous though it is, but the harm is done nonetheless. Refusing to form my conscience properly, refusing to assimilate the moral direction God gives me points me toward spiritual harm and possibly even toward spiritual self-destruction.

Acting Prudently

Of equal importance to forming our consciences properly is knowing how to apply our understanding to concrete circumstances here and now. This is the task of the virtue of prudence. Applying the wrong principles in a concrete situation can be as destructive as not having any principles at all. Persons who try to fit principles and circumstances together incorrectly often end up in a simplistic moral legalism or with a bad case of scruples.

For example, is it right for me to take the offer of a new job with a different employer? In order to answer that question I must analyze the implications of the job which has been offered. Am I able to do the work? Is it honest work? How will I be better off than I am now? And what about my present employer? What obligations am I under? What wider contexts should be considered? How will new employment affect my friendships? My religious life? My family? Inherent in all these questions are moral values dealing with honesty, faithfulness, fraternal charity, religion and probably some others as well. I must try to apply all these principles to the concrete circumstances of the job offer and reach a decision.

Only I can make that decision; but, when I make it, I am responsible for it. If I have done my best possible job of judging, I have made a conscientious decision; I am in good conscience. If I have knowingly rejected or disregarded some moral principles or values, I have made a wrong decision and my conscience will reproach me for the decision as I reflect on it later.

Freedom of Conscience

Where does freedom of conscience fit into all this? *Freedom of conscience* refers to two different things.

First, since my conscience is the final judge of what I must or may do, nobody may make that judgment for me. I must determine how the categories of right and wrong apply to my circumstances here and now. Nobody else may impose his or her judgment on my conscience. Because I am responsible for the judgment, my conscience is and must be "free." This does not mean that I am free to do whatever I want, or to establish and follow any moral principles I wish. I cannot disregard church teaching if I do not like or understand it, or because it is demanding. But the judgment I finally make comes from within me and, in that sense, is free.

The second meaning of freedom of conscience concerns the relationship of civil society to my religious beliefs. My conscience is "free" because no civil government has the right to tell me what I must believe or what religion I am to practice. Those decisions, inherently personal, must be made in the context of a person's relationship with God, not in the context of civil law. Used in this sense, freedom of conscience is the equivalent of freedom of religion.

Fundamentally, conscience is the way in which I discover where goodness and growth and maturity lie here and now, the way I assimilate and make my own God's love for this individual human creature.

But our conscience is never completely and definitively formed. Nor is its exercise ever completely effortless. There is always room for greater moral maturity, always room for more refined moral choices. That's why conscience remains a tough issue.

Discussion Questions

1. In what aspects of my life do I make judgments of conscience?

2. Is it ever possible or appropriate to second-guess someone else's conscientious decisions?

3. What specific resources are available to me to assist in the proper formation of my conscience?

For Further Reading

Catechism of the Catholic Church, 1776–1802.

Pope John Paul II, Encyclical Letter *Veritatis Splendor,* 1993, nos. 54–64 (*Origins* 23:18).

Conclusion

Our Christian life is certainly much more than a series of tough issues, but tough issues are unavoidable. And as we face them, we find ourselves asking questions: Why are there so many tough issues? Why is it such a struggle to live up to what God expects of us? Why is God's will so hard to understand sometimes? How can a loving God demand so much of us? Why do things seem to go so badly so often?

The effort, the sense of struggle and the failures we experience originate from at least three tensions.

Individual vs. Communal

The first tension is between individual and community, between the one and the many. Each of us has an instinct to look after ourselves. Self-preservation is a basic drive.

In addition to this healthy, natural instinct for survival, we also experience an inclination to selfishness, to an unhealthy self-seeking which we have inherited from the sinfulness of our human ancestors. It is a distortion of our original human drives. Our instincts and their distortions tell us to take care of our own needs—and take care of them first. Almost spontaneously we put ourselves before everyone else. Yet the needs of the community may make it necessary for me to put my personal wants aside, temporarily or even permanently.

These two demands pull us in different directions. They cause tension. How is a childless couple to reconcile the desire to conceive with a reverence for the processes of human generation? How are the sexual inclinations of the homosexual to be reconciled with the universal purposes of human sexuality? How can my desire to live a full and comfortable life be reconciled with the unjust aspects of the social system which offer me the comforts I seek? The individual and the community are in tension, and tension causes struggle and pain.

Present vs. Future

Another difficult truth—and tension—emerges in this context. God does not call us to ultimate personal happiness and total fulfillment here and now. We await the fullness of life in a future not yet fully disclosed to us. So we live in the tension between the world *already here* and the world *still to come*.

Our faith teaches us that God's love for us cannot be totally expressed in the present circumstances of this world, that the best is still in the future. Individual sacrifice here and now is therefore not the last word. The heavy demands which faith and morality sometimes seem to make on us do not render faith and morality irrelevant or unrealistic or destructive. Individual suffering and failure here and now do not mean that God has abandoned us or that our human existence is without meaning, any more than success and temporal well-being are a sign of holiness and ultimate success.

Society's voices tell us that our every desire deserves immediate satisfaction, that lack of comforts is an injustice perpetrated on us. Our society claims that the real meaning of life lies not in struggle toward ideals but in a state of pleasant self-sufficiency. Our society tells us that success comes from the right breaks and our own hard effort. These are pleasant things to hear. The trouble is they are not true. Our faith teaches us otherwise. Our faith teaches us that discomfort is not the final outrage, that a wrong kind of self-sufficiency can destroy us, that whatever is of real value in life is the result not of achievement but of gift.

The voices we hear at every moment from our culture are difficult to disregard. It is hard to accept the demands of self-sacrifice, to carry out our pledges of faithfulness, to accept the suffering which comes with caring about other human beings, to struggle to understand the import of the church's teachings when these voices keep telling us that we are wasting our time. They try to convince us that we are foolish to wait for "pie in the sky" when we can have limitless sex and drugs and other good things here and now.

Human vs. Divine

A third cause of tension arises from the very generosity of God. Sometimes our life is hard because God wants to give us so much. He wants to share his very life with us. He wants to give us eternal happiness with him, he wants to enable us to look on the world the way he does, he wants us to love one another the way he loves us, he wants us to respect ourselves as he respects us. God gives us the ability to accept all these gifts, but acceptance is not without its demands.

God's gifts may demand that we allow some certain satisfactions to take second place, that we extend ourselves in ways which seem to exceed our capacities, that we conduct ourselves in ways that seem to non-believers to be excessively severe, or unintelligent or even harmful. Our refusal to countenance abortion, our willingness to oppose an unjust war, our respect for the life of a criminal, our faithfulness to what we perceive to be the will of the historical Jesus—all of this stems from God's abundant gifts. Many people whose lives touch ours may judge us unrealistic—even foolish. Sometimes we may be tempted to make those same judgments ourselves.

Yet God's gifts can never destroy us. If they make things tough for us, it is because they put us in tension with our human limitations.

In the final analysis, the effort we exert, the pain we suffer and the difficulties we face are the price of growth: growth from selfishness toward generosity, from mindless participation in an unhealthy society toward moral maturity, from the limitations of humanity toward sharing the life of God.

Quite simply, God calls us to be like himself. Our model is the Lord Jesus whose life was a life of total self-giving to his heavenly father. His life evoked rejection and suffering and execution as a criminal, but ended in resurrection and glory. God gives us Jesus'life to live when we are baptized. Everything from then on is a matter of growth, of growth into what Jesus was, of growth into what Jesus is.

As we face tough issues, our Christianity calls us beyond merely surviving moral dilemmas unscathed. Our vocation is to be faithful to what God is calling us to be. Our task is to grow in Christ.

As we face the tough issues, we must ask ourselves where to find the goodness of God in them, where God's will lies. We must know the larger context from which the "rules" arise. We must know not only what the church teaches, but also how church teaching strives to express God's call to live out our likeness to the Lord Jesus. We must know not only what moral directives demand of us but also what moral directives say about God's Word, God's plan, God's call, God's humanity —and what all this says about growing in the life of Christ.

We hear many voices as we struggle to mature. Some are loud, some are soft. Their variety makes listening difficult. Sorting them out is tough. But there is one voice we must be sure to hear if we are to grow to authentic maturity: the voice of God, speaking through Christ and his church. To each and to all God says, "I love you."

Discussion Questions

1. What moral issues do I find the toughest? Why?

2. What tensions do I encounter most often in my moral decision making?

3. Which of God's gifts do I find most burdensome? Most welcome?